Featherstone

# 50

## fantastic ideas for
# tuff trays

SALLY WRIGHT

Featherstone
An imprint of Bloomsbury Publishing Plc

50 Bedford Square
London
WC1B 3DP
UK

1385 Broadway
New York
NY 10018
USA

www.bloomsbury.com

FEATHERSTONE and the Feather logo are trademarks of Bloomsbury Publishing Plc

First published in Great Britain 2018

A catalogue record for this book is available from the British Library.

ISBN
PB: 978-1-4729-5428-2
ePDF: 978-1-4729-5429-9

4 6 8 10 9 7 5 3

Printed and bound in India by Replika Press Pvt. Ltd.

This book is produced using paper that is made from wood grown in managed, sustainable forests.
It is natural, renewable and recyclable. The logging and manufacturing processes conform to the
environmental regulations of the country of origin.

To find out more about our authors and books visit www.bloomsbury.com. Here you will find extracts,
author interviews, details of forthcoming events and the option to sign up for our newsletters.

# Contents

# Introduction

Children learn through their play. Sensory and messy play stimulate a child's senses and are great ways for children to explore, think scientifically and be creative. To provide this type of play, most early years settings will have some form of tuff tray equipment. This could range from the 'Tuff Spot Trays' sold by educational outlets to a simple builders' cement mixing tray, a potting tray or a muddy boots tray. A tuff tray is a shallow tray with a flat surface and a small surrounding lip or edge which allows for maximum access and minimum spillage. The tuff tray is easy to clean and store which makes it an ideal resource for childminders, pack-away settings, nurseries and schools alike.

For the purposes of this book, I will use the term 'tuff tray' in relation to the popular octagonal-shaped trays. These have eight sides to promote group activity and can be purchased in a variety of colours. Some of these trays have height adjustable frames, but they can also be used on the floor or on top of a table. Size and style will really depend on your setting and the requirements of your children. Each activity in this book can simply be adapted to suit your needs and available resources.

The popularity of such a versatile early years staple resource has resulted in an array of beautiful creations by practitioners and parents which are then shared online. However, these are often unrealistic for busy settings to recreate; a tuff tray activity should not be a complicated task to prepare. Whilst these masterpieces are fine if you have the time and inclination, they can also be a little off-putting for the less creative among us and offer no more learning opportunities than the tray which has been put together in five minutes or less.

The key to preparing an effective tuff tray activity is to ask ourselves these key questions:

Why are we doing this tuff tray activity?

- Is it linked to our children's interest?
- Is this tuff tray activity an enhancement for something we are learning about?
- Is this part of our continuous provision?

How will the children benefit from this tuff tray activity?

- Will the children acquire new skills or develop existing skills?
- Can the children lead their own play and investigation?
- Does this tuff tray activity link to a child's developmental needs?

The tuff tray can provide so many opportunities for exploration and discovery. It is our role to ensure that the tuff tray is prepared in such a way that it will engage and motivate our children to investigate and learn. One of the most important strategies for the effective use of a tuff tray is to allow the children to lead and explore without predetermined expectations of how activities must unfold. Even the best prepared activities very rarely go to plan. If you keep this in mind, you will never be disappointed with the outcomes of a tuff tray exploration.

The ideas you will find in this book are very simple to prepare, with many of the materials readily available in most early years provision or easily sourced from your own kitchen cupboard, collected from nature or through some resourceful scavenging.

I have brought together some of my favourite activities which will hopefully illustrate how simple it can be to provide fantastic learning opportunities using the tuff tray. I hope you will be inspired to prepare something new, exciting and fantastic for your little learners.

## Let's talk safety

All tuff tray activities should be child-led. However, the tuff tray should always be closely supervised by an adult to avoid accidents.

- As many of the tuff tray activities are based on sensory and messy play opportunities, it is always a good idea to have hand washing facilities close by.

- Food is used for sensory exploration and not consumption, although I cannot guarantee there will not be a little sampling! My advice is always to err on the side of caution and make sure all items are sufficiently cleaned using anti-bacterial products before the activity begins.

 Activities which include food products should be prepared with careful consideration to food allergies. Look out for this symbol on the relevant pages.

 Some items may be unsuitable for children with sensitive skin or allergies; to prevent reactions, always ensure you check the ingredients of any detergents and soaps, etc. Look out for this symbol on the relevant pages.

 Using natural resources or small parts can be choke hazards so it is important to ensure you are comfortable that the tuff tray activity is age appropriate. You may need to remind little ones not to put things into their mouths. Look out for this symbol on the relevant pages.

 Using water in your activities is a measured risk. There is always a risk of drowning, even when the water is not very deep. There will usually be a lot of spillage, so standby with a mop. If you can, water play activities are better done outdoors on grass to prevent slipping hazards.

## The structure of the book

The pages are all organised in the same way. Before you start any activity, read through everything on the page so you are familiar with the whole activity and what you might need to plan in advance.

**What you need** lists the resources required for the activity. These are likely to be readily available in most settings or can be bought/made easily.

**What to do** tells you step-by-step what you need to do to compete the activity.

The **Health & Safety** tips are often obvious, but safety can't be overstressed. In many cases, there are no specific hazards involved in completing the activity, and your usual health and safety measures should be enough. In others, there are particular issues to be noted and addressed.

**Taking it forward** gives ideas for additional activities on the same theme, or for developing the activity further. These will be particularly useful for things that have gone especially well or where children show a real interest. In many cases, they use the same resources, and in every case, they have been designed to extend learning and broaden the children's experiences.

Finally, **What's in it for the children?** tells you (and others) briefly how the suggested activities contribute to learning.

# The tea party

## Water play

## What you need:

- Cups and saucers
- Teapots
- Teabags
- Warm water
- Teaspoons
- Sponges

### Top tip ⭐

Use metal pots and sturdy cups (not your best China) to begin with whilst assessing the children's ability to handle the equipment.

### ➕ Health & Safety

Breakages will not be as frequent as you might expect, but be on guard and ready to clear up broken crockery. Standing the tuff tray on foam mats may help minimise this risk.

## What to do:

1. Set up the cups and saucers around the edge of the tuff tray.

2. Put the teapots in the centre of the tuff tray but not too far away for the children to access. Fill them with a small amount of water to begin with. Remember that a full teapot may be too heavy for some children to control. By putting the teapots in the centre of the tuff tray, you are allowing the children the time to pick up and make predictions about how to hold and balance the teapot before introducing the cups.

3. Show the children how to make a cup of tea. Using language such as 'first we add the tea bag' and 'then we add the water' can be a good way to incorporate mathematical language into the children's play.

4. Model how to tip the teapot back and forth to control the water flow and how to use the teaspoons to mash the teabag gently.

5. Using fruit tea bags will give the children another sensory experience as they are strongly scented and also create interesting colours.

6. Use the sponges to collect up spilt water and transfer it back into the pots so the activity can be explored again.

7. Once you have modelled how to make tea, it is important to allow the children to explore freely.

### Taking it forward

- Why not have a taste? Make fresh and hygienically prepared (caffeine free) fruit tea. Let the tea cool for a little while and ask the children to 'pour the tea' for you to drink.

### What's in it for the children?

Offering real equipment for the children to explore will give them a sense of responsibility and help them link their play to real life experiences. Allowing the children to explore 'making tea' can meet many learning needs such as the mathematical concepts of exploring volume and capacity, learning about sequence and following instructions, along with developing hand-eye coordination and upper arm muscle development whilst pouring.

# Washing up

## Water play

## What you need:

- Something that needs washing!
- Water bowls
- Mild soap bars
- Soap dispensers
- Dish brushes
- Sponges
- Towels

## Top tip

Tie string loops around the tuff tray using the canopy holes or around the frame and attach towels for easy access.

### Taking it forward

- Talk about sequencing and the order of events required for thorough washing. If washing dolls, for example, you may want to go through the process of how you give them a bath: get wet, use soap, rinse and then dry.
- Ask the children to help with washing up at home.
- Progress on to using real pots and pans to develop life skills.

### What's in it for the children?

Children love washing up and they also like to feel as though they are contributing. Washing up can be seen as a 'job' from which they will get a sense of accomplishment.

## What to do:

**WATER hazard!**  **SKIN allergy!**

1. Finding things to wash is the first challenge. This should be linked to your children's interests – a child who loves wheels will enjoy cleaning the cars more than the dinosaurs. However, if you have some particularly grubby resources, there is no harm in multi-tasking. We always 'bathe the babies' at the beginning of each term, simply because they need it.

2. Find bowls which are deep enough to get a fair amount of water in but not too deep that the children cannot reach into them. Provide a selection of dish brushes and sponges.

3. The frame on the tuff tray can be lowered if the bowls are too high for little ones to reach into when they're placed on the tuff tray.

4. Add mild soap, either bars or liquid depending on the children you are working with. Add both to differentiate for those who find the pump dispensers tricky.

5. Provide towels or tea towels for drying the resources.

# Rock pool play
Water play

## What you need:

- Rocks
- Shells
- Driftwood
- Sand
- Water
- Seaweed (use cut up plastic plants or aquarium plants)
- Small world rock pool creatures, e.g. crabs and starfish
- Small buckets or nets

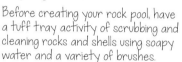

## Top tip ⭐

Before creating your rock pool, have a tuff tray activity of scrubbing and cleaning rocks and shells using soapy water and a variety of brushes.

### Taking it forward

- Visit the seaside with the children to collect more shells, rocks and driftwood and experience a real rock pool exploration.
- Ask your families to collect seaside treasures whilst on their holidays.

### What's in it for the children?

This activity promotes communication and language development. It will help children develop a wider understanding of the world. This activity is effective as part of your continuous provision after holiday breaks and can often prompt children to share their experiences through the small world play enhancement. Alternatively, use this activity to show the children who may not have the opportunity to visit the seaside what rock pool exploration might look like.

## What to do:

1. Before using this tuff tray enhancement, you should ensure children know what a rock pool is. Look in books, at online photographs, or plan a visit to the beach or a local aquarium.

2. Provide all of the resources and allow the children to create the rock pool using the knowledge they have gained though their earlier experiences.

3. Play a game of hide and seek whereby one person hides the sea creatures and the others must search to find them.

4. Allow the children to explore the rock pool and support them by using language and questions linked to rock pool exploration.

### ➕ Health & Safety

Model how to search and explore carefully in order to avoid bashed fingers and sandy eyes. Always supervise the children around water.

# Ball blowing
**Water play**

## What you need:

- Antibacterial spray
- Small jug of water (enough to cover the tuff tray with a thin layer of water)
- Light balls such as ping pong balls or ball pit balls
- Straws

## What to do:

1. Ensure the tuff tray is cleaned with antibacterial spray.
2. Add the water and the balls.
3. As each child approaches the activity, give them a clean straw and explain that it must be thrown away after use.
4. Show the children how they can blow through the straws to move the balls across the water.
5. Explain that the water is not for drinking.
6. Encourage children to blow the balls to each other from each side of the tuff tray.

## Top tip ⭐

Test the children have understood the concept of 'blowing' before putting their straws in the water. Ask them to blow through the straws onto your hands to test that the breath is coming through.

### Taking it forward

- Once the children have developed the skill of blowing, add a little washing up liquid or soap to the water to make bubbles.

### What's in it for the children?

Blowing through a straw is believed to help with speech development and may be useful for children who need additional support with their spoken language. There is also a great sense of achievement when children succeed at a task and can observe the cause and effect of an action so this in turn will help to build self-awareness and self-esteem.

# Water station
Water play

## What you need:

- Water trays
- Buckets
- Tubs
- Pipes
- Water dispensers
- Scoops
- Funnels
- Poster paint
- Baby bubble bath (sensitive and unscented)

## Top tip ★

Put the children in swimwear (where appropriate). Alternatively, use splash suits or be prepared to change clothes.

### Taking it forward

- Try using a variety of temperatures from hot (only as hot as is safe for your children) to cold.
- Add ice to explore the melting process.
- Use the station idea to explore different mediums such as sand, foam, rice and grains.

### What's in it for the children?

Creating a water station will help children develop social skills as they work alongside each other to negotiate space and resources. Water play promotes physical development through pouring, squirting, stirring and squeezing and helps to develop hand–eye coordination.

## What to do:

1. Set up a water station as a production line so that the children can work along it, transferring and transporting the water along the station in different trays and containers.

2. Set the water stations at different heights to encourage problem solving when transporting.

3. Add pipes for the children to explore the direction and flow of the water.

4. Include things which require problem-solving skills such as water dispensers, taps and water pumps, as well as scoops and funnels.

5. Adding a small amount of poster paint into the water will promote exploration in mixing and making potions.

6. Adding bubble bath to the water can offer another sensory experience.

7. Allow the children to explore and experiment freely.

# Herb exploration
Food play

## What you need:

- Malleable material (homemade play dough, moon dough or bread dough)
- Chopping boards
- Rolling pins
- Scissors
- Cupcake cases
- A variety of herbs, potted or picked from the garden

## What to do:

1. Choose and prepare your malleable material. You may wish to add a selection of different types of dough to explore.

2. Create 'work stations' around the tuff tray using trays or chopping boards. This is always advised when using equipment such as scissors to help the adults keep track of where they are.

3. Each station should include malleable material, rolling pins, scissors and cupcake cases, providing the children with everything they will need during their exploration.

4. Place herbs around the tuff tray so that everyone has access. Choose herbs with strong and distinctive smells such as mint, coriander and basil.

5. Depending on the age of the children, adults need to model how to cut the herbs effectively. Younger children can simply pick the herbs.

6. Discuss with the children the different smells and textures.

7. Promote creativity, investigation and exploration. Children may cut the herbs and add to the malleable material to create 'herb cakes' or roll out the herby mixture to make 'pancakes'.

## Top tip ⭐

This can also be an opportunity to allow the children to make their own dough material. Making their own dough will ensure that the children have a vested interest in the next steps of the activity and give them a sense of ownership and achievement.

## ✚ Health & Safety

Using scissors can run the risk of children snipping fingers or possibly even worse; many new hair styles have been created in the early years setting! Supervision is required. If you have a child who is a 'taster', then the moon dough is probably not the best option. Instead opt for an edible play dough alternative.

### Taking it forward

- Grow your own herbs with the children. Teach children the names of the herbs and how they smell.

- Have a guessing game whereby the children smell the different herbs and try to identify them.

- Why not try adding dried herbs to malleable materials for further exploration?

### What's in it for the children?

This is a multi-sensory activity which could also engage children who may be reluctant to access the craft table or practise their cutting skills. Using herbs for cutting as opposed to the more traditional paper gives children the freedom to be creative and make mistakes without any pressure.

# Peas, glorious peas

Food play

## What you need:

- Chalk
- Frozen peas
- Straws

## Top tip

There is only so much blowing the children will be able to do. To get the most out of this activity, have resources available for further exploration, such as containers for emptying and filling or potato mashers for pea smashing (once the peas begin to defrost).

### Taking it forward

- Include a variety of frozen, fresh and dried peas for the children to make comparisons and investigate the differences between them. Cook and taste the different peas.

- Why not add other vegetable such as carrots and discuss why they do not move as easily?

### What's in it for the children?

Blowing through straws is a great exercise for teaching children how to control their breath. Having this skill and control will also help with speech development. Using the mashers for making pea mush is good for gross motor skills and will help to develop upper arm muscles.

### ✚ Health & Safety

Frozen peas are inviting and sensory in their own right but could fit perfectly up a small nostril or into a neighbour's ear. Close observation required for this activity.

## What to do:

1. Draw a simple circle in the centre of the tuff tray using chalk. This is going to be the target for the blown peas.

2. Add the frozen peas around the edge of tuff tray. Allow the children to explore how the peas feel at this point and use language such as 'frozen' and later 'defrosted'. This is also an opportunity to discuss keeping food fresh, being healthy and the value of food.

3. Give each child an individual straw and explain that they must not share with each other (to avoid cross-contamination of germs).

4. Model how to blow the peas and instruct the children to aim for the target. Lots of encouragement and cheering will help the children to reach the target.

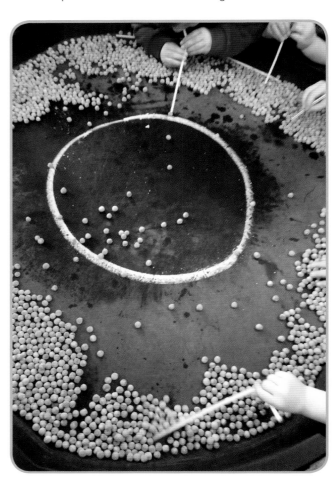

# Banana chopping
Food play

## What you need:

- Chopping boards
- Child-friendly plastic knives or safety knives
- Bananas

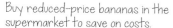

**Top tip** ⭐

Buy reduced-price bananas in the supermarket to save on costs.

### Taking it forward

- Teach the children that knives can be for spreading too by incorporating an activity which includes spreading and cutting such as sandwich making.
- Once the children have mastered the skill of cutting safely, why not make the activity more challenging and get the children to cut something harder, such as a cucumber? For this activity 'real knives' may be required.

### What's in it for the children?

By allowing the children to engage in risky play, such as using knives, we are promoting self-regulation and self-control; the consequences of misusing the equipment becomes very real and personal to the child.

### ✚ Health & Safety

Because of the use of knives, plastic or real, careful consideration must be given to health and safety of the children and those around. Close supervision and modelling is required to ensure the children are using the equipment safely and that they stay at their chopping stations.

## What to do:

1. Place the chopping boards around the tuff tray to create stations for the children to have their own designated space.
2. Allocate one knife per board making sure you count them out, ensuring on clear up that all are returned.
3. Place the bananas (unpeeled) in the centre of the tuff tray.
4. As this is food play using something which is quite inviting for the children to nibble, I would suggest hand washing before the children are allowed to explore.
5. Model to the children how to open the banana and how to chop safely, being careful of fingers.
6. Allow the children to explore freely.

# Potato mashing
Food play

## What you need:

- Large potatoes
- Potato peelers
- Pan
- Water
- Potato mashers

## Top tip

Differentiate the activity by cooking the potatoes to different levels of softness to make the task more challenging.

### Taking it forward

- Why not allow the children to add paint to the mashed potatoes to explore mixing colours and changing the consistency?
- Try potato tasting (obviously not using the same batch!).
- Before or after this activity, you could explore where potatoes come from and plant your own.

### What's in it for the children?

Apart from being a sensory activity which will stimulate a child's senses such as touch, smell, taste, sight, hearing, balance and movement, children can also learn about cause and effect. This activity helps to develop an understanding of how things change during the cooking process. The mashing is a great gross motor exercise, too.

### Health & Safety

Ensure potatoes are completely cooled through to the middle before using them.

## What to do:

1. Peel the potatoes. This is a great part of the process to allow the children to either observe or take part in. There are various products on the market to allow the children to do this safely.

2. Show or explain to the children how you will cook the potatoes in boiling water until they soften.

3. Allow the potatoes to cool before using them.

4. Place potatoes around the tuff tray with the mashers.

5. Add some raw potatoes for the children to make comparisons between the two consistencies. This is a good opportunity to discuss the concepts of 'soft' and 'hard' with the children.

6. Let the children explore the potatoes freely. They may need an adult to model how the potato can be mashed with the mashers. Some may prefer to use their hands. This is a sensory activity and however the children choose to play should be encouraged.

7. Once the potatoes are all mashed, the children can mould and manipulate the mash into shapes and models. They can then re-mash their designs.

# Cooked and raw
Food play

## What you need:

- Chopping boards
- Plastic knives or safety knives
- Cooked vegetables
- Raw vegetables

## Top tip ⭐

Do not overload the younger children with too many vegetables; explore one vegetable at a time.

### Taking it forward

- Why not explore frozen, dried or even tinned vegetables and make comparisons?
- Grow your own vegetables to eventually harvest, cook and eat.
- Visit a working farm with the children to pick crops directly from the field to consolidate the knowledge gained.

### What's in it for the children?

This is a sensory activity that requires good hand–eye coordination. Teaching the children about where food comes from, how it looks in its natural form and how it tastes and feels once cooked will give the children a deeper understanding of the food cycle and the world around them.

### ✚ Health & Safety

Using knives safely, plastic or the safety variety, should be modelled before the activity starts.

## What to do:

 **CHOKE hazard!** **FOOD allergy!**

1. Before we explored this tuff tray activity, we visited a farm where we were able to pick our own vegetables from the field. We looked at the vegetables in the farm shop and then later cooked some.

2. Set up stations using chopping boards and knives which are suitable for the children you are working with. Younger children may prefer to explore with their hands and older children may be able to use the knives independently (with supervision).

3. Provide a selection of cooked and raw vegetables in the centre of the tuff tray. Include vegetables that have been picked straight from the farm and also ones which are washed and sold in the supermarket for the children to make comparisons. Some children may only have experienced what 'cooked vegetables' look like and will be surprised to see the difference in their appearance when raw.

4. Allow the children to explore the different textures and make comparisons through manipulating and cutting them.

# Handa's surprise
## Supporting books

## What you need:

- *Handa's Surprise* storybook
- Antibacterial spray
- Chopping boards
- Knives
- Baskets
- Bananas
- Guava
- Oranges
- Mangoes
- Pineapples
- Avocado
- Passion fruit
- Tangerines
- Labels for fruit

## What to do:

1. Read the story with the children and talk about the different fruits. Ask the children if they know what each of the fruits look like and if they have ever tasted them. Share the story a few times before doing this tuff tray activity so that the children become curious about the fruits.

2. Clean the tuff tray and chopping boards with antibacterial products as although this is not a food preparation activity, the children can be invited to taste the fruits.

3. Set up work stations with chopping boards and knives for the children to use to explore the fruits.

4. Arrange the fruits in the baskets and display the tuff tray in a way which will invite the children to explore. Adding labels will also incorporate literacy into the play which can be built upon depending on the age of the children. Can they find the word in the story? Which animal ate the fruit?

5. Ensure the children wash their hands before approaching the tuff tray.

6. Allow the children to explore freely using their hands or with the knives provided. The supervising adult should support them with their exploration, model how to use the equipment safely and promote conversations around the fruits and the story when appropriate.

## Top tip ⭐

Before starting the activity, why not engage the children's curiosity by playing a guessing game about the different fruits: what is the fruit's name? What will it look like inside? How will it taste?

### Taking it forward

- Why not re-enact some of the other parts of the Handa's Surprise story? Try carrying the basket of tangerines on your head.

### What's in it for the children?

Using hands-on sensory play will help children make sense of the story. They will be able to understand more about the fruits being spoken about in the story. How many of the children will know what a guava looks and feels like, or even an avocado? There is the potential for language development and the adults should work closely with the children during this activity.

### ✚ Health & Safety

Because of the use of knives, plastic or real, careful consideration must be given to health and safety of the children and those around them. Close supervision and modelling is required to ensure the children are using the equipment safely and that they stay at their chopping stations.

# Dinosaurs love underpants

## What you need:

- *Dinosaurs Love Underpants* storybook
- Small world dinosaurs
- Underpants (the smallest you can find!)
- Rocks
- Sticks
- Sand
- Tissue paper

## Top tip ⭐

Use underpants which link to the children's interest. This will give them another topic of converstaion and will encourage them to explore. We used Spiderman ones for our superhero enthusiasts!

### Taking it forward

- If the children are engaged in this activity, why not try the *Aliens Love Underpants* story next?

### What's in it for the children?

This is a literacy enriched activity with a little added humour to engage the children's interest. Using props to support a book will help the children make more sense of the story and help to demonstrate certain concepts which are hard to visualise, for example 'why T-Rex can't reach his legs to put his underpants on'. ('Because of his short arms'.)

## What to do:

1. Introduce the story to the children before they experience the tuff tray enhancement.

2. Create and design the tuff tray using the dinosaurs, the underpants and any bits you have found to add such as rocks, sticks, sand and tissue paper.

3. Once the children have calmed down from the hysterical concept of underpants in the tuff tray, an adult should read the story and act out the scenes.

4. Use the dinosaurs which are mentioned in the book and ask the children to find the matching dinosaurs. If they do not know which they are, then show them what the dinosaurs looks like using the book as a reference.

5. Allow the children to then play freely and explore the dinosaurs and underpants.

6. Be prepared to read the story over and over again!

# Duck in the truck

Supporting books

## What you need:

- *Duck in the Truck* storybook
- Small world animals from the story: duck, frog, goat, sheep
- Truck
- Boat
- Mud
- Blue tissue paper
- Chalk

## Top tip ⭐

Don't worry too much about how the tuff tray looks, the focus is on incorporating the rhyming words during play.

## What to do:

1. This activity is about promoting the rhyming words used in the story. As the children are exploring the small world enhancement, use the stories rhyming words: 'duck in a truck', 'stuck in the muck', 'sheep in a jeep' and so on.

2. Create a small world scene from the story using mud for land and torn blue tissue paper for water.

3. Use chalk to mark out and label what each thing is. These labels can be referred to depending on the age of the children to explore rhyme further.

4. Read the story whilst the children play and allow them to fill in the missing word, for example: 'here comes the duck in a...?'

### Taking it forward

- Why not take the small world play outdoors in the mud to explore further?

### What's in it for the children?

Rhyme is important for children to learn as part of their language development and is an aspect of their phonemic awareness. It is linked to how children listen, identify, and change the sounds in spoken language. Rhyming is the groundwork of learning how to read and write. For early years children, the repetition of the rhymes will also promote listening and understanding.

# Three little pigs

## What you need:

- *Three Little Pigs* storybook
- Straw or hay
- Sticks
- Wooden bricks
- Play dough or clay
- Three little pigs
- One big bad wolf

## Top tip ⭐

Use pet bedding for the straw which can be purchased in very small quantities at a pet shop.

### Taking it forward

- Why not try to construct on a larger scale? Use large blocks to build a 'brick house', build a stick den or purchase bales of straw and construct a house!

### What's in it for the children?

During small world play, children can use their imagination; it's an opportunity to build on their language skills including vocabulary and understanding. Expressive language skills can also be explored in this story as the children can narrate their play. Positional language may be used as children put the pigs inside the houses, on top or underneath. The children will change the story as their play evolves, and they will have their own ideas which will promote independent play and encourage self-confidence.

## What to do:

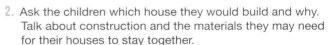

1. Read the story to the children beforehand.

2. Ask the children which house they would build and why. Talk about construction and the materials they may need for their houses to stay together.

3. Place stations around the tuff tray with each of the materials; straw, sticks and bricks.

4. Add play dough or clay to each of the stations for the children to use when constructing their houses.

5. Suggest the children build a house for each of the pigs and then role play to see if the big bad wolf can blow them down.

6. Allow the children to explore freely and create their own constructions.

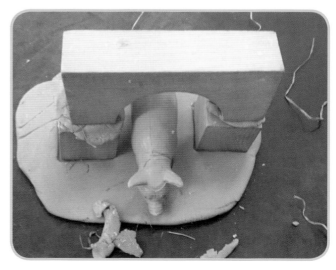

# Bear hunt

## What you need:

- *We're Going on a Bear Hunt* storybook
- Small trays
- Tissue paper (blue and green)
- Artificial grass pieces (or tissue paper)
- Sticks
- Rocks
- Foliage
- Compost
- Fake snow (cotton wool or homemade snow)
- Small world people
- Doll's house bed
- Small world bear
- Cave (any tunnel covered in dark fabric)
- Small world woodland and Arctic animals (optional)

### Taking it forward

- Go outside and recreate the bear hunt for the children to experience themselves. Use tuff trays for the water, mud and snow (you could use frozen rice instead of snow).

### What's in it for the children?

Providing the props to allow the children to explore the characters and themes of a book enables them to make sense of the events in the story. This is also a great way to engage the children who find it difficult to sit and listen to a book. Inevitably, the tuff tray sections will end up looking like a mess as snow gets mixed in with grass and so on. Remember this is okay – the children can still learn through this sensory exploration.

## What to do:

1. Prepare the tuff tray so that it includes distinct sections which represent each of the pages and experiences illustrated in the book.

2. An adult should support the tuff tray exploration by reading the story as the children engage with the small world activity.

3. The children can act out the scenes as they take the small world people around each of the sensory areas.

4. Encourage the children to talk about how each area feels and see if the children can recall the story themselves.

### Top tip ⭐

Make your own snow by mixing cornflour with shaving foam. It feels cold to touch!

## What you need:

- Warm water
- Salt
- Poster paint or food colouring
- Spray bottles
- Snow
- Spoons
- Pipettes

## What to do:

1. Prepare a mixture of warm water and salt. Make sure the water is warm enough to dissolve the salt otherwise it will clog the spray bottles.

2. Add either a small amount of poster paint or some food colouring to the mixture.

3. Shake the mixture well. Making the colour solution is a great activity to include the children in and will give them a more thorough understanding of the activity when they experience the mixture melting the snow.

4. Ensure nozzles on spray bottles are on 'mist' setting and not 'jet', otherwise the colours will shoot beyond the tuff tray.

5. Collect snow and place it in the tuff tray. This can be an exciting activity in itself.

6. Model with the children how to use the spray bottles and be prepared to hold the bottles steady whilst they develop this tricky skill (age dependent). Talk with the children about the effect the coloured mixture has on the snow, including how the salt helps the melting process.

7. Experiment with mark making and colour mixing.

8. Have resources at the ready for the children to enhance their play further, such as spoons, pipettes and more poster paint solution.

## Top tip ⭐

If you can't wait for snow or have no chance of getting any, you can improvise and use cotton wool sheets or homemade fake snow.

## ➕ Health & Safety

Although the snow and solution are not harmful, it is not recommended that the children sample them. Close supervision is required.

## Taking it forward

- Take the children outside and explore on a bigger canvas. The jet setting on the spray bottles is good for this activity.

- Explore ice and experiment with different ways in which to melt it.

- Differentiate the activity by using water pistols or empty washing up bottles depending on the skill level of the children.

## What's in it for the children?

Using a spray bottle is great for developing and strengthening hand muscles. Aiming the sprays onto a small surface area is really good for coordination, making predictions and estimating cause and effect. Waiting until the snow becomes water will help the children understand more fully about snow and the melting process, and will provide an altogether new sensory tuff tray experience.

# Petal potion

## What you need:

- Chopping boards
- Wooden sticks
- Pipettes
- Fruit tea
- Hair conditioner or lotions (child friendly)
- Small bowls
- Petals (garden petals or supermarket flowers)

## Top tip ⭐

Ask your local florist for flower debris rather than using fresh flower petals.

### Taking it forward

- Provide bottles for the children to transfer their potions into to take home for window displays. This works better without the thickening agents (e.g. conditioner).

### What's in it for the children?

This activity is unlikely to go as you have planned, but the children will get a sense of awe, wonder and enjoyment from potion making. This is a sensory activity which is about combining and exploring scientifically. There are opportunities for language development, and conversations to be had about colours, smells and textures.

## What to do:

1. Prepare working stations using chopping boards or trays.
2. Each station should have all the individual tools required for creating petal potion – this ensures the children will have what is needed to create freely.
3. Prepare fruit teas for the children to use as a base for their potions – this is a sensory exploration which should be filled with different scents and textures.
4. Use conditioners and lotions to add texture to their potions. Putting these items into bowls rather than just using the bottles will give the children a chance to spread it further, although squeezing conditioner and body lotion is a fantastic activity in itself.
5. Place petals around the work stations for easy access.
6. Allow the children to mix and create freely.

# Nature's process art

## What you need:

- Natural and seasonal debris
- Cardboard
- Glue (optional)

## What to do:

1. Collect pieces of natural foliage or debris from a nature walk or the garden and place in the centre of the tuff tray.

2. Cut small pieces of cardboard and place around the edge of the tuff tray.

3. Glue is an optional extra although it's not essential as the art can be transient.

4. Allow the children to freely create their masterpieces.

5. Encourage the children to return the natural loose parts and start their pictures over again.

### Top tip ★

This is an activity for free expression. You could model your own design, but remember to allow the children to enjoy the process.

### Taking it forward

- Use photo frames or mirror surfaces as a canvas to extend the activity.

- Use other loose parts to promote transient art.

### What's in it for the children?

This kind of activity gives the children freedom to manipulate, explore and experiment with shapes and patterns. The focus is on the process of the activity as opposed to producing an end product. This removes any pressure or expectations on the children and will enhance their emotional wellbeing.

### ➕ Health & Safety

Ensure all natural pieces are safe, non-poisonous and not of a size which could be a choke hazard.

# Autumnal soup

## What you need:

- Natural resources (sticks, shells or rocks)
- Autumnal resources (leaves, conkers, acorns and pine cones)
- Pots and pans
- Bowls
- Spoons
- Water
- Cornflour

## Top tip ⭐

Try to source deep pans which are heavy and sturdy as this will minimise the risk of the pans being tipped out, although it will not completely eliminate the risk.

### Taking it forward

- Collect rain water to use for the soup and use this as an opportunity to talk about conservation.
- Read the story 'Stone Soup' to support and extend the activity.

### What's in it for the children?

This is an open-ended exploration which will promote curiosity and wonder. Children will enjoy the sensory experience of mixing and being able to develop their own unique creations.

## What to do:

1. Take the children on an autumn walk to collect the natural treasure and talk about what you find.

2. When preparing the tuff tray, think about the age and size of the children and ensure that the tray is at a height whereby the children can look into the pans as they create their soup.

3. Put the collected items in bowls and place pans and spoons around the tuff tray.

4. Pour water into the pans. Allow the children to add the 'ingredients' as they wish and to explore what happens during the process.

5. To incorporate mathematical concepts, talk about how the water changes when certain materials are added, for example adding the rocks to their soup will make the water rise and taking them out again will lower the water level.

6. Adding the cornflour to the mix will thicken the water, therefore enhancing the process and extending the play.

# Cherry blossom chopping

## What you need:

- Cherry blossom
- Chopping boards
- Selection of scissors
- Play dough

## Top tip ⭐

Although you intend this activity to be about scissor skills, the children may take it in a completely different direction – I've seen potion making, dough modelling and scattering blossom confetti. This kind of open-ended and child-led play should be allowed to unfold naturally without interruption.

### Taking it forward

- Use other seasonal foliage such as a Christmas tree or autumn branches.
- Explore the growth cycle of the cherry blossom throughout the seasons.

### What's in it for the children?

Not all children will access the scissors if they are generally to be found in the 'crafting area'. Bringing scissors into a tuff tray activity for children to experiment with can be engaging and captivating for some children, especially those who rarely visit the crafting area.

## What to do:

1. Collect the blossom with the children. The flowers only last on the trees for a couple of weeks in late spring and many can be found on the ground for the children to collect.

2. Set up chopping board stations each with a scissor selection for the children to experiment with.

3. Place some malleable play dough material on each board. The consistency of the play dough should match the age and stage of development of the children. For younger children, a regular play dough recipe will suffice; for older children who need something more challenging, try something which is harder to manipulate such as a clay or tougher dough to encourage the use and development of the hand muscles.

4. Put the cherry blossom in the middle so the children can freely help themselves.

5. Cherry blossom is an ideal material to use to practise scissor skills as the branches and shoots are easy to cut and manipulate.

### ➕ Health & Safety

Although cherry blossom is not poisonous, it is not advisable for children to eat it so supervision is required.

# Number cars

## What you need:

- Chalk
- Permanent maker
- Cars
- Cardboard tubes
- Cardboard box
- Sticky tape

## Top tip ⭐

Use strong tape to secure tubes and ramps. For the ramp, hook the cardboard over the frame before putting the tuff tray in place for extra hold. Tape the ramp to the floor also to hold firmly in position.

## What to do:

1. You will need two tuff trays for this activity. Using the chalk, write numbers in 'parking bays' on one of the tuff trays.

2. Use permanent marker to write numbers onto cars. White or light coloured vehicles work best. If you do not want to mark them permanently, you can use stickers.

3. Lower or heighten one tuff tray and attach cardboard tubes between the two so that they are at an angle.

4. Open a large box and attach it to the tuff trays to make a ramp between the two. This can be decorated to look like a road to enhance the small world play.

5. Model with the children how to match the correct cars into the parking bays.

6. Allow the children to explore freely but also talk and work alongside them, if appropriate, to provide challenge and problem-solving opportunities.

7. Help them to theorise about what may happen; for example, 'I wonder where the car will go if I send it down the big tube?'

8. Older children could turn this into a game. They could add up the number on their car with the number in the parking space where the cars end up and see who has the most points.

## Taking it forward

- Why not incorporate other items into the exploration to promote comparisons and making estimations? For example, include ping pong balls and ask the children to predict whether the car or the call will travel fastest down the tube. You could also add a variety of shapes and item of differing weights for comparing similarities and differences.

## What's in it for the children?

There are so many opportunities for the children to learn mathematically and to explore and investigate scientifically in this activity. Firstly, we are introducing numbers into the children's play for them to familiarise themselves with to improve recognition and recall; there are also opportunities for sorting, categorising, matching, estimating, and exploring distance and speed.

### ✚ Health & Safety

Flying cars at the end of the cardboard ramp could potentially be a hazard so position your trays wisely.

# Potato weighing

## Promoting mathematics

## What you need:

- Potatoes of varying sizes (from large baking potatoes to small salad potatoes)
- Bowls
- Weights
- Rocks
- Balance scales

## What to do:

FOOD allergy !

1. Ensure the tuff tray is at a height whereby children will be able to clearly observe the quantities on the scales – you may need to lower the height a little.

2. Sort the potatoes into large, medium and small sizes and put them into bowls. The children can help you with this.

3. Add weights and rocks. The rocks are for the children to use one mass to compare weight as opposed to several weights. This will help the children to understand that 'more' does not represent 'heavier'. One rock will need lots of potatoes to balance it. This can be differentiated and made more accurate using weights once the children have acquired the skills of balancing.

4. Show the children how the scales work. Traditional scales and balancing educational scales are best for the children to explore.

## Top tip

Why not peel and cook the potatoes afterwards and use for a mashing sensory activity? (See Potato mashing, page 16.)

### What's in it for the children?

There are lots of mathematical and investigative opportunities in this activity. For the younger children, incorporate words such as 'big', 'small', 'heavy' and 'light'; for the older children, use 'making estimations', 'comparisons' and 'predictions' along with 'sizing', 'categorising' and 'weighing'.

### Taking it forward

- Try weighing different items.
- Use digital scales and weigh out exact measures. Compare these on the scales.

# Matching and sizing tins

Promoting mathematics

## Top tip ⭐

Collect unusual and interesting containers from car boot sales, charity shops or Grandma's cupboards. Use some 'recognisable' containers so the children can identify with the activity.

### Taking it forward

- Once the children have learnt the skill of matching the lids to the containers, add items of varying sizes which will only fit in specific sized containers. This will promote mathematical inquiry. Many children love enclosing items and enjoy the act of opening and closing containers as part of their preferred approach to learning.

- For children who enjoy posting, why not create a 'posting tuff tray' which explores size.

### What's in it for the children?

There are so many mathematical and problem-solving opportunities presented with this activity which can be easily differentiated for the children's age and stage of development and to different objectives. This activity also can link in with children's schemas such as enclosing, enveloping or transporting schemas.

## What to do:

1. Take all the lids off the containers.

2. Place containers on one side of the tuff tray and lids on another.

3. Explain to the children that each container has a lid which will fit it perfectly.

4. You may need to start by demonstrating this activity with the children depending on their age and stage of development.

5. Use lots of praise and encouragement as the children successfully match the corresponding lids with the containers.

6. Talk about size and the different shapes of the containers.

7. Discuss the labelling of the containers and 'guess' what may have originally been stored in them.

8. Once all the lids have been matched, count how many you have in total.

9. See if you can make that number smaller by seeing if you can fit smaller tins into larger tins. This task is great for problem solving, estimating and making predictions.

## ➕ Health & Safety

Ensure all containers have been thoroughly cleaned, especially if sourced from car boot sales and charity shops. A wash in soapy water and a wipe of anti-bacterial spray will suffice. Check that there are no unsuspecting sharp edges on 'used tins' by carefully running your hand around them and check after every use.

# Transferring and transporting

**Promoting mathematics**

## What you need:

- Two tuff trays with frames
- Pipes
- Tubes
- Cable ties
- Tape
- Bowls
- Fabric
- Foil
- Cotton wool
- Scoops
- Jugs
- Spoons
- Rice and pasta

## What to do:

1. Detach one of the tuff trays from its frame.

2. Attach the pipes and tubes to the tuff tray frame using cable ties and tape. This is tricky so you may need another adult to help. If you haven't got a tuff tray frame, look around your setting and get creative, maybe an upturned table will work.

3. Attach the pipes at varying heights to provide a diversity of levels. You want the highest pipe to push the children's abilities, promoting hand–eye coordination and the physical challenge of stretching and reaching.

4. Add a lower pipe so that the children can observe the materials travelling down the pipe.

5. Place the frame into the tuff tray to catch the medium which is being transported.

6. The children will naturally climb into the tuff tray to explore the tubes from different angles so make sure the frame is secure and cannot be easily pushed over.

7. Place bowls underneath the tubes to catch the transferable medium.

8. On the second tuff tray, provide materials so the children can experiment with blocking the flow of the medium, for example using pieces of material, foil or cotton wool to create a blockage.

9. Add scoops, jugs and spoons for the children to experiment with pouring and transferring.

10. Allow the children to explore, experiment and investigate freely.

### Top tip ⭐

Add some free-standing pipes and tubes for the children to create their own paths for the medium.

34

## Taking it forward

- Explore and experiment with different mediums using the vertical pipes.

- This would be a great outdoor activity. Why not experiment with bird seeds as a medium so any surplus spillages can be used to feed the birds?

- Get creative and experiment by positioning the tubes diagonally and horizontally.

## What's in it for the children?

Children who have moved on from the filling, pouring and emptying stage of materials exploration will be able to experiment with how mediums move when deposited in different directions (in this case, through vertical transportation). The rice and pasta will offer a pleasant sound as they travel which will encourage the play. The children will be gaining an understanding of mathematical concepts such as direction, height, shape, space, volume and capacity.

*50 fantastic ideas for tuff trays*

# Once I caught a fish alive ...

Promoting mathematics

## What you need:

- Magnetic fishing set
- Pipe cleaners
- 4 Colanders
- Blue tissue paper
- A large bowl

## Top tip

Magnetic fishing sets can be purchased online from most educational suppliers or toy shops.

### Taking it forward

- Explore materials where the children must predict which items are magnetic and which are not.

- Add non-magnetic fish into the trays or create a tray specifically for exploring and comparing materials.

### What's in it for the children?

There are many opportunities to develop children's knowledge and understanding of the world through exploration and investigation. This activity also gives you the chance to incorporate number language into the children's play. Using a familiar rhyme will help the children to make sense of the tuff tray enhancement along with developing early number sense. Children can learn to recognise the number of objects in small groups, a mental skill which can be developed even before counting with understanding.

### Health & Safety

Magnets can be harmful to children if swallowed so ensure all magnetic equipment is safe and fit for purpose!

## What to do:

1. Sing the nursery rhyme 'Once I caught a fish alive' with the children.

2. Thread the pipe cleaners through the colanders to create a 'seaweed' effect. The pipe cleaners make it difficult for the children to 'hook' the magnetic fish as the string from the rod will get caught in the pipe cleaners. This means the children require a steady hand and some problem-solving skills to hook a fish.

3. Shred up the tissue paper to represent the water and put in the colanders.

4. Sprinkle the fish into the colanders and give each child a fishing rod.

5. For younger children, simply encourage them to negotiate hooking the fish and transferring it into the large bowl.

6. For older children who are beginning to understand numbers and quantity, start with 5 fish in the large bowl and then assign the colanders numbers 1-4. In number 1, the children should add 1 fish, in number 2, 2 fish and so on. This will help the children begin to develop and understanding of quantity.

# Threading cereals
Promoting literacy

## What you need:

- Cereal hoops
- Bowls
- Straws
- Sticky tack
- Pipe cleaners
- Shoelaces

## What to do:

1. Ensure there are bowls of cereal hoops available around the tuff tray to support right-handed and left-handed preferences.

2. Take a bendy straw and place sticky tack around the bend. Stick the straw to the board so the longest section in pointing towards the ceiling. This provides another dimension to the threading which takes a steady, skilful hand and careful coordination.

3. Set out pipe cleaners and shoelaces for additional challenge.

4. Model how to thread the cereal onto the different resources, explaining that the hoops will fall off the ends if carried around.

### Top tip ⭐

Pipe cleaners are the easiest thing to begin with whilst the children are learning the skill of threading.

### Taking it forward

- Why not tie the items together (pipe cleaners or shoelaces) and hang them outside as bird feeders?

### What's in it for the children?

This activity takes skill and determination. For a child to thread hoops onto pipe cleaners, they must stay focused for extended periods of time. The activity will promote the development of the thumb and the index finger in preparation for mark making and writing.

# Oranges and lemons hand strengthening

Promoting literacy

## What you need:

- Pans
- Water
- Oranges
- Lemons
- Knives
- Bottles
- Jugs
- Funnels
- Sparkling water

## What to do:

1. Set up the tuff tray with pans and fill two with tap water about half way up. Remember to lower the tuff tray for smaller children as they may not be able to reach or see into the pans.

2. Cut the oranges and lemons in half. Cutting fruit is a fantastic activity to include the children in depending on age and stage of development.

3. Add other equipment around the tuff tray such as bottles, jugs for pouring and transferring, and funnels.

4. Wait until just before the children are going to begin exploring and then add the sparkling water for extra fizz and sparkle. Make comparisons between the two liquids.

5. Model how we can transform the water into orange or lemon juice by squeezing the fruits into the water. It takes considerable skill and hand strength to produce any liquid from the fruit.

6. Once the children have created their 'juice', they can go on to transfer it into the bottles using the jugs and funnels.

## Top tip ⭐

Use sponges to collect the spilled water and squeeze back into the pans. Not only does it help manage the spillage, it is fantastic for working the hand muscles too.

## ✚ Health & Safety

Do not let the children consume the mixtures. Ensure pips are removed from fruits to eliminate the risk of eating them.

## Taking it forward

- Why not try using fruit juicers for squeezing the juice out? This will involve a different kind of muscle use by pushing down and manipulating the fruit around to produce liquid.

- Make your own lemonade for consumption.

## What's in it for the children?

This activity will promote actions that strengthen hand and upper arm muscles. This development is required to ensure that children are prepared physically to become operative mark makers and writers. The activity is also very sensory and will encourage children to explore further if this is their preferred approach to learning. It has the potential to engage the more reluctant mark makers to explore and investigate whilst developing those important physical requirements.

50 fantastic ideas for tuff trays

# Making marks

## What you need:

- Salt and glitter mix
- Ice scraper
- Shaving foam
- Sponges
- Paint brushes
- Water
- Chalks
- Chalk pens
- Sticks

## Top tip ⭐

Prepare mark making tuff trays using a variety of heights, from the floor to the highest setting on the stand, as well as vertical tuff trays, to promote a diverse collection of physical challenges.

### Taking it forward

- Once the children have become confident in experimenting with making marks using a variety of mediums, you may wish to incorporate more complex tools and materials.

- Why not try using a quill pen for writing in a small layer of sand for developing the fine motor skills?

- Add challenging malleable materials such as modelling clay. You will need to adapt the activities to suit the children you work with and their learning requirements.

### What's in it for the children?

This is a creative and sensory exercise where the children can explore freely and securely without expectations of how things should be done. This will give them confidence to explore and experiment with mark making.

## What to do:

1. Add your chosen medium to the tuff tray for the children to explore.

2. Model with the children how to make marks using the tools provided.

3. Experiment with how to clear the tuff tray to make a fresh canvas. For example, a shake of the tuff tray when using the salt/glitter will freshen it up for more mark making; use an ice scraper to smooth out shaving foam; or add sponges and wet paint brushes for washing away chalk.

4. Ensure the children have the opportunity to make small marks (for example, using chalk pens) along with really big marks (for example, using the shaving foam).

5. Encourage the children to stretch across the tuff tray to promote physical development and the use of important core muscles needed for effective mark making and writing.

### ✚ Health & Safety

The hazards would be dependent on the tools and medium used. All tuff trays should be supervised.

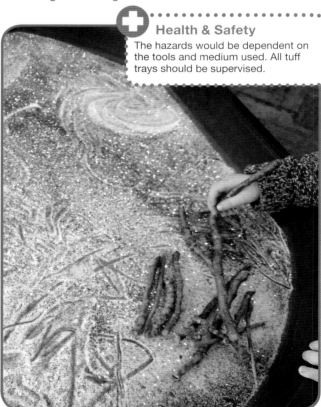

# Squeezy targets
## Promoting literacy

## What you need:

- Coloured chalks
- Empty washing up liquid bottles
- Water

## Top tip ⭐

Ask your family and friends to start saving washing up bottles.

### Taking it forward

- Once the children have cleared the chalk, give them chalks to create their own marks to 'squirt away'.

- Depending on the age of the children, it may be easier to lay the tuff tray flat for this activity.

- Have a squeezy competition by marking various distances from the target to challenge children to squeeze harder.

### What's in it for the children?

This activity is great for working the hand muscles and for the upper shoulders as the children have to lift and tilt the bottle and then squeeze firmly and release to get the water out. This kind of aim and fire activity will also appeal to children who are interested in weapon play and can be adapted to follow their interests.

### ✚ Health & Safety

Ensure the tuff tray is secured when in the upright position.

## What to do:

1. Using different coloured chalks, make a shooting target on the tuff tray.

2. Fill the washing up liquid bottles with water.

3. Explain to the children that if they squeeze the bottles with two hands, they will be able to squirt the water onto the target.

4. Stand the tuff tray on its side and lean it next to something to keep it from falling over.

5. Begin with allowing the children to explore and experiment with the bottles. The activity will promote hand-eye coordination and it takes strength and balance to be able to successfully hit the targets on the tuff tray.

6. Once the children have experimented, they can be asked to aim for particular colours.

# Outdoor reading nook
## Promoting literacy

## What you need:

- 7 (approx.) garden canes
- String
- Fabric
- Cushions
- Books

## What to do:

1. Place the canes around the inside rim of the tuff tray. Ask the children to hold them for you.

2. Tie the top with string and secure the canes in place.

3. Ask the children to weave the fabric through the canes, leaving an opening at the front.

4. Add cushions for comfort.

5. Place books within easy reach.

6. Explain to the children that this space is for only one or two children to access at one time and is for reading and looking at books.

7. Allow the children to access the reading nook as they please.

## Top tip

Instead of balancing the canes around the rim, place planters around the tuff tray and pop the canes inside for added security.

### Taking it forward

- Why not create an indoor reading nook by covering the tuff tray frame with a blanket and then adding torches for further intrigue?

### What's in it for the children?

Some children prefer to play and learn outdoors, especially boys. The children will get a sense of accomplishment through helping to construct their reading nook which will give them a sense of ownership and encourage them to use it. They will be curious to investigate and to take a turn going into their construction. This will result in a higher level of engagement and interest in exploring books.

### ✚ Health & Safety

Ensure canes are fixed securely to prevent the frame tipping over.

50 fantastic ideas for tuff trays

# Hot chocolate

Sensory play

## What you need:

- Hot chocolate powder (white, milk and dark chocolate)
- Mugs
- Mini marshmallows
- Sprinkles
- Squirty cream
- Warm water in jugs
- Spoons
- Old sponges

### Taking it forward

- Allow the children to taste some freshly made hot chocolate – an especially nice treat on a cold and wet day!

- Use flavoured chocolates such as orange, toffee and mint to extend the sensory exploration further.

- Add chocolate powder to different malleable materials such as homemade play dough or a gloopy mixture of cornflour and water.

### What's in it for the children?

The children will enjoy the sensory experience of playing with chocolate scented materials – who wouldn't! The activity will allow the children to talk about what they can smell. There are lots of beneficial outcomes from this activity through sequencing, experimenting, mixing, pouring and the skill needed for using the squirty cream is great for promoting strong fingers, fine motor skills and hand–eye coordination.

## What to do:

**FOOD allergy !**  **CHOKE hazard !**  **WATER hazard !**

1. Place all the items on the tuff tray. Use real equipment so that the activity is representative of true life. Depending on the age of the children, you may want to model how to make an actual hot chocolate drink and suggest that the children follow a sequence.

2. Explain that the hot chocolate they are creating is not for drinking.

3. Allow the children to create and explore freely with the variety of flavours, smells and textures. Some children will mix a thick paste and others may miss out adding the powder altogether and opt for just squirting cream.

4. Use old sponges to gather spilt liquid to reuse during the activity. These sponges will be better thrown into the bin afterwards!

### Top tip ⭐

There is no better sound than that of a metal spoon stirring liquid in a real mug, this cannot be imitated using plastic play resources.

# Bread play dough
## Sensory play

## What you need:

- Chopping board or tray stations
- Bowls
- Spoons
- Soap dispensers (cleaned and filled with fresh water)
- Bread mix
- Water

## What to do:

1. Set out each station with a chopping board, bowls, spoons and a water dispenser.

2. The bread mix already has yeast in so it only requires water to create an elasticated dough-type malleable material. You can experiment with white or brown mixtures and different flavoured bread mixtures.

3. Allow the children to experiment with how much water they need to add to the mix to create a dough.

4. You may wish to prepare a dough as an example for the children to see what they can create if they get the combination correct.

## Top tip ★

Use the soap dispensers to promote hand muscle development by pumping the water out. This also avoids lots of water being poured into the mix straight away.

### Taking it forward

- Why not experiment with different recipes for making dough?

- For older children, add instructions for quantities and sequence.

### What's in it for the children?

This is a sensory exploration which promotes independence, perseverance and problem solving. It is about the children exploring smells, textures and different ingredients and for them to investigate what happens when liquid is added to the flour. As the children become more skilled, the consistency of their dough will improve.

# Soapy suds
Sensory play

## What you need:

- Empty soap dispensers
- Water
- Sponges
- Bars of sensitive child-friendly soaps
- Fresh water for hand washing

## Top tip

Add scents and flavours to the water to make this more of a sensory experience.

### Taking it forward

- You can differentiate the activity by using spray bottles for the water; these are great for developing muscles and hand-eye coordination.
- Why not add colour using powder paint or food colouring and pipettes to create rainbow suds?

### What's in it for the children?

The children will experience a lovely sensory activity while exploring cause and effect. Squeezing sponges and working the soap dispensers are excellent activities for developing strong hand muscles, which in turn helps with emerging mark making skills.

### ✚ Health & Safety

Use child sensitive soap and ensure that there is a bowl of water for regular rinsing of the hands. Don't allow the children to rub their eyes with soapy hands.

## What to do:

**SKIN allergy !**

1. Fill the empty dispensers with water.
2. Add sponges and bars of soap to the tuff tray along with the filled dispensers.
3. You may need to model with the children how to create the soap suds by squirting water onto the sponges and rubbing it with the soap bar, then squeezing and moving the sponges around the tuff tray.
4. Allow the children to explore freely.

# Sensory bottles

## What you need:

- A variety of plastic bottles and containers
- Grains
- Pulses
- Other store cupboard leftovers
- Containers e.g. egg cups, jugs and bottles
- Funnels
- Spoons

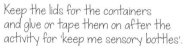

## Top tip ⭐

Keep the lids for the containers and glue or tape them on after the activity for 'keep me sensory bottles'.

### Taking it forward

- Explore with different mediums such as liquids, sand, stones or anything which will create curiosity.
- For the 'Keep me' sensory bottles, try adding small and interesting loose parts which you may not ordinarily allow the children to access so they can observe and explore these safely.

### What's in it for the children?

The children will enjoy filling, emptying and pouring. The focus of this activity is the problem-solving skills needed to transfer a medium from one place and into another – such as into a bottle or container. The activity requires perseverance and skills for the children to successfully be able to transfer the medium. The sensory bottles created afterwards are a by-product and are not the objective. There are lots of mathematical possibilities in this activity along with sensory opportunities.

## What to do:

1. Position the containers in the centre of the tuff tray so that the children can see the variety of shapes and sizes on offer before choosing.

2. Place the various grains and pulses in bowls around the tuff tray.

3. Show the children (if required) how to transfer the mixture into the containers using the funnels and spoons.

4. An adult can support mathematical enquiry by discussing size, volume and capacity while the children are working. Ask questions such as, 'Which has more mixture, the egg cup or the bottle?' or 'How much mixture will you need to fill this container?'.

5. Encourage the children to explore the sensory aspects of the textures and experience the sound of the grains falling. You may wish to create a 'keep me sensory bottle' for the children after they finish exploring.

# Celery chopping

**Sensory play**

## What you need:

- Chopping boards
- Scissors (palmer and safety scissors)
- Knives (child friendly)
- Celery

**Top tip** ⭐

Chop the ends of the celery bunch and use it for printing. They make excellent prints which look like flowers.

### Taking it forward

- Experiment with cutting other items for sensory exploration and developing scissor skills. Cabbage leaves, herbs, flowers, soft branches or stems and green beans/peas are all good options.

### What's in it for the children?

If the children are engaged in a task which has meaning with an 'end result', they are more likely to persist with the challenge unlike when they are given free choice to promote scissor skills at a craft table. This sensory exploration will encourage children to participate through the rewarding sounds and smells produced and it will also promote further investigation.

### ➕ Health & Safety

Caution is required when using scissors or knives.

## What to do:

**CHOKE hazard !**  **FOOD allergy !**

1. Use the chopping boards to create stations which will ensure the children stand at a safe distance away from each other and enable the adults to keep a close eye on equipment.

2. Provide the children with a variety of scissors which suit their stage of development.

3. The celery is crunchy when cut and releases a strong aroma which will encourage the children to explore and investigate.

4. Allow the children to access the activity freely and offer support where required. Some children may need to be shown how to use the equipment safely.

5. Children will create their own style for cutting. Some will prefer to cut big pieces and others will chop very small. This could be used as an opportunity to discuss sizing.

# Chopstick challenge

## What you need:

- Bowls
- Chopsticks
- Fruits
- Vegetables
- Tweezers
- Tongs

## Top tip ★

Add Chinese decorations to the tuff tray to add curiosity and intrigue.

### Taking it forward

- Why not add noodles, grains and peas to the tuff tray for the children to explore and experiment with?

### What's in it for the children?

The chopstick challenge is a fun activity which can be used to support conversation with the children about different cultures and help to develop their understanding of the world. Chopsticks can be tricky for children to use but the concentration and hand muscles required will be useful as they move on to mark making.

## What to do:

 **CHOKE hazard!** **FOOD allergy!**

1. Set up the bowls and chopsticks around the edge of the tuff tray.

2. Chop the fruit and vegetables into large chunks and place them in bowls in the centre of the tuff tray. Choose fruit and vegetables with different textures and shapes for the children to explore.

3. Model with the children how to use the chopsticks. This is a very tricky concept – training chopsticks are useful, if you have them. Also provide tools which are easier to use such as large tweezers and tongs.

4. Challenge the children to take as many items from the central bowls as they can. Who can collect the most? What is the smallest and largest piece they can successfully carry?

5. The activity can be used to provoke a discussion about Chinese New Year. Adults should talk about Chinese food and culture and explain how they celebrate the New Year. The depth of conversation will be dependent on the age and interest of the children.

6. For older children, you can count the items in each bowl that the children have successfully moved using the chopsticks or tweezers.

6. Prompt the children to theorise about which item will be easiest to transfer and then put their theory to the test.

# Poppies

Festivals, celebrations and reflections

## What you need:

- Sand
- Red glitter
- Small world army set
- Natural resources such as rocks and stones
- Poppies

## Top tip

Although purchasing poppies does go to a very good cause, you can also make them using crêpe-paper and a black marker.

## Taking it forward

- Explore this topic further by investigating other people who help us and to whom we should give thanks.
- Read poems and stories which talk about remembrance and being thankful.

## What's in it for the children?

The children will explore the tuff tray in much the same way in which they would any small world enhancement. The idea for this particular tuff tray activity is to open a conversation about poppies and remembrance through the child's play and to give them a deeper understanding of the wider world. Before implementing this tuff tray activity, you should take into consideration the setting and the cohort of children within it. Remember that children consolidate their existing knowledge and make sense of the world through their play. This kind of play can help children work through things they do not understand.

## What to do:

1. Sprinkle a small scattering of sand onto the tuff tray as a base. You may wish to add red glitter to the sand to represent the 'poppy fields'.

2. Create your tuff tray provocation using small world army resources.

3. Use natural resources as a sensory enrichment to the tuff tray for the children to explore.

4. Scatter poppies around the tuff tray.

5. Many children will have seen their parents, grandparents and teachers wearing paper poppies. As the children begin to access the activity, an adult can support their investigation by inquiring about their knowledge of the poppies.

6. Allow the children to play freely and support the activity by incorporating language and discussion around war, poppies, remembrance and thanks.

# Wrapping presents

Festivals, celebrations and reflections

## What you need:

- Wrapping paper cut into manageable sizes
- Sticky tape
- Tape dispensers
- Scissors
- Gift tags
- Ribbons
- Pencils
- Boxes to wrap

## What to do:

1. This activity can promote conversation about Christmas, a Christian celebration where the sharing of gifts is very common.

2. Set out the materials on the tuff tray.

3. Allow the children to wrap and explore freely.

4. For older children, you can model how to wrap a present and the sequence to follow. Use this opportunity to discuss why people send Christmas presents to each other.

5. Encourage the children to write on the gift tags and discuss what gifts they would send and to whom. This will promote creativity and imagination.

### Top tip ★

For younger children, you can attach scissors to string and tie them onto the tuff tray to avoid them getting lost or carried away to another part of the setting.

### Taking it forward

- Create a station where the children can deliver their presents.
- Incorporate more complex shapes for the children to wrap.
- Play a game of 'guess what's wrapped'.

### What's in it for the children?

Children love enclosing things and will enjoy the process of wrapping. They will have a sense of achievement when completing the task. They will also enjoy sharing their gifts as they may have experienced giving and receiving gifts before.

### ✚ Health & Safety

Scissors can be a hazard if left unsupervised.

# Kahk cookie mixture

Festivals, celebrations and reflections

## What you need:

- Semolina flour
- Water
- Bowls
- Jugs
- Spoons

## Top tip

Semolina flour can be purchased from most supermarkets.

### Taking it forward

- Why not try a taster session and purchase some ready-made Kahk for the children to sample?

- Follow a recipe to bake your own Kahk cookies.

### What's in it for the children?

The aim of the activity is to invite discussion and conversation about Eid and the wider world; it is also a sensory activity which promotes scientific enquiry, early mathematics and gross motor skills. The tuff tray exploration won't result in edible cookies, but offers the opportunity to start discussions about other cultures.

## What to do:

1. This activity is a sensory activity to promote conversation about Eid al-Fitr celebrations which is a Muslim holiday to mark the end of Ramadan, the Islamic month of fasting. Families and friends often gift each other with a traditional dessert called Kahk which is a cookie type dessert. This dish is enjoyed during the Ramadan feasts.

2. Set up the tuff tray with semolina flour, water, bowls and spoons.

3. This a 'hands on' activity. Allow the children to explore freely using their hands and enjoy the sensory experience the flour and water will create.

4. Provide spoons for those children who prefer not to explore with their hands and let them enjoy the process of mixing.

5. Support the children's explorations by explaining that these are some of the ingredients used to make Kahk, discussing what Kahk is and how it may taste.

6. Use this as an opportunity to open conversations about Eid and the celebrations surrounding it.

7. For older children, you may add weighing scales and instructions for them to follow along with other ingredients which may be used in the Kahk recipe.

# Rangoli patterns
Festivals, celebrations and reflections

## What you need:
- Coloured sand in a variety of shades

## Top tip ⭐
Show the children how to pour the sand gently from their hands before they begin to create their designs.

## Taking it forward
- Use different mediums to explore pattern making, such as coloured rice. (Put white rice in a food bag, a little antibacterial gel and a squirt of poster paint, move rice around and then lay out onto a flat surface to dry.)
- Why not add piping bags filled with sand or rice for the children to use to make their patterns?

## What's in it for the children?
Creating and recognising patterns is a good way to develop children's mathematical awareness which can be explored further depending on the age of the children. However, the children will largely be drawn in by the bright colours and the patterns. This activity is an excellent opportunity to discuss Diwali and the use of Rangoli patterns in the celebrations surrounding these festivals.

## What to do:
1. First show the children lots of photos of Rangoli patterns created to celebrate the festival of Diwali.
2. Speak to the children about how Diwali is the Hindu 'festival of lights' which celebrates the victory of good over evil and, for some, the New Year. Explain how the Hindu people decorate their homes and temples by drawing patterns outside, in the hope that the goddess Lakshmi will see them and visit their homes.
3. An adult may make an example of a pattern for them to look at and explore in the tuff tray.
4. Have a selection of coloured sands available which can be placed on a table close by for the adults and children to access freely.
5. Older children can make their own patterns using their hands by gently sprinkling the sand onto the tuff tray. Younger children will enjoy exploring the sand and patterns with their hands.

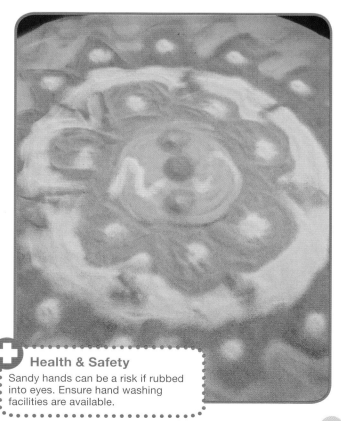

## ✚ Health & Safety
Sandy hands can be a risk if rubbed into eyes. Ensure hand washing facilities are available.

# Pumpkin train tunnels

## Small world enhancements

## What you need:

- Pumpkins
- Carving set or knife
- Marker pen
- Train set

## Top tip ⭐

If pumpkins are not in season, try using watermelons.

### Taking it forward

- You could use this enhancement to explore tunnels further. Read the story *The Train Ride* by June Crebbin and Stephen Lambertto and talk about reflections when the trains go through a dark tunnel.

### What's in it for the children?

Children will enjoy having a different element brought into their usual small world play which will promote sensory exploration. This will appeal to the children who enjoy enclosing. It creates problem-solving opportunities as the children try to move the trains through the tunnels and must negotiate the small space and adapt their technique.

## What to do:

**FOOD allergy!**

1. This is a great way to use up leftover pumpkins and allow the children to engage in a sensory exploration whilst playing with small world resources.

2. Cut off the top of the pumpkin and allow the children to scoop out the insides. This in itself is a lovely sensory activity for the children to explore.

3. Draw a tunnel shape on the side of the pumpkin as a guide for cutting out.

4. Cut out an arch on either side of the pumpkin to create the tunnels opening.

5. Cut 'windows' into the side of the pumpkins so that the children can observe the train moving through the tunnel during their play. They can also use the windows for negotiating the train through the tunnel if required, so make them big enough for a small hand to fit through.

6. Place your tunnels in the tuff tray and construct a track running through them.

7. Allow the children to play freely and explore the small world enhancement.

# Frozen excavations
## Small world enhancements

## What you need:

- Small world resources (linked to your children's interest or current topic)
- Freezer-safe containers
- Water
- Paint
- Glitter
- Space in your freezer
- Pipettes
- Warm salt water
- Hammers
- Brushes
- Torches
- Magnifying glasses

## Top tip

Use a solution of warm salt water in spray bottle to help the children melt the ice.

### Taking it forward

- Add more things for the children to 'excavate' alongside the ice such as jelly, shaving foam or paint.
- Freeze natural resources such as rocks, sticks and pinecones along with the small world resources.

### What's in it for the children?

This is a sensory activity which will require the children to problem solve, change strategies and demonstrate perseverance to complete the task.

### ✚ Health & Safety

Using tools such as hammers with children requires supervision and guidance.

## What to do:

1. Place some of the small world items in containers and add water.
2. You can add glitter or poster paint at this stage to colour and sparkle the water to add interest and intrigue.
3. Place in the freezer overnight.
4. Run the frozen containers under warm water to release the ice blocks and ensure that there are no sharp edges. If there are rough or sharp parts, run the ice under warm water to smooth it out.
5. Using the warm water, you can make holes in ice chunks to start the children off in their excavation.
6. Set up the tuff tray small world enhancement.
7. Provide tools for helping the children to chip away or melt the ice such as pipettes and warm water, small hammers, tools for scraping and brushes.
8. Add torches and magnifiers for the children to explore and investigate what is in the ice and examine their progress.
9. As the activity moves forward, you may wish to add hot water to help dissolve the ice so that the children can see an end result, especially if you are short of time. Alternatively, you can leave the activity out until the ice melts naturally so that the children can experience the whole process.

# Searching for minibeasts

## What you need:

- Seasonal outdoor natural objects (twigs, leaves, stones, pinecones, conkers and flowers)
- Minibeast small world selection
- Magnifying glasses
- Small containers

### Taking it forward

- Make a list of the creatures and then take the children on a real minibeast hunt to look for the same insects and spiders.
- Children enjoy creating their small world play independently so start with an empty tray and just provide the loose parts for the children to choose from.

### What's in it for the children?

Using small world enhancements can be a good way to engage children in conversation and for them to talk about their existing knowledge and learn new things. Some children may be fearful of minibeasts and playing with the creatures in small world is an opportunity to help them to make sense of their fear and possibly overcome it.

### Health & Safety

The children should be taught that some real minibeasts can bite or sting and they should not be handled unless supervised by an adult.

## What to do:

1. Scatter your natural resources in the tuff tray.

2. Add the minibeasts. These can be hidden underneath the natural pieces. Why not ask the children to look away in a game of 'hide and seek' and then see how many they can find?

3. Show the children how to use the magnifying glass and explore how the minibeasts look bigger through it.

4. Talk to the children about what they can see and the minibeasts they find. Examine them and discuss the features of each minibeast.

5. Use pots to make collections of what they find. Insects in one, spiders in the other, and so on. Do the children know how to differentiate between the two?

6. Compare the minibeasts and use questions to promote curiosity and wonder – for example, how many can fly and how many cannot? Where do you think they live?

### Top tip ⭐

Encourage the children to handle the minibeasts with care as they would if they were real. This will help them to understand how we should respect and be careful with minibeasts.

# Harvest
## Small world enhancements

## What you need:

- Sand
- Compost
- Small vegetables (sprouts, radish, new potatoes, cabbage leaves or carrots)
- Small world diggers/tractors

## Top tip ⭐

Gourds are good to use in a harvest tuff tray as they are hardy and last a long time. They can be used over and over for the children to explore fully.

## What to do:

1. Mix the sand and compost together and sprinkle a shallow covering in the tuff tray.
2. Line up the vegetables.
3. Add the diggers or tractors.
4. Allow the children to play freely.
5. Adults can support the play by talking to the children about harvest, about growing vegetables and about the farmers who collect the crops using the tractors.
6. Encourage the children to move the vegetables by filling, scooping and transporting.

### Taking it forward

- If you can, visit a farm where the children can see the crop fields and the tractors harvesting.
- The activity could also link in with the 'Cooked and raw' tuff tray activity (see page 17).

### What's in it for the children?

There are opportunities for promoting language development and incorporating mathematical awareness through sorting and comparing. More importantly, this tuff tray activity allows children to develop a deeper understanding of the world as the they learn about farming and harvesting food.

# Small world jumble

## Small world enhancements

## What you need:

- A broad collection of small world pieces
- Natural materials such as rocks, sticks and shells (optional)
- Fake grass pieces and sand (optional)
- Tissue paper (optional)

## Top tip

For fake grass, ask local gardeners and landscapers for off-cuts or turf samples.

### Taking it forward

- Add construction materials to the small world enhancements or malleable materials for the children to combine this type of play with problem-solving and physical development.
- Provide the resources on a separate table and allow the children to create the small world enhancement as they wish using the materials they choose.

### What's in it for the children?

Having the freedom to lead their own play is the best way for children to learn. Providing them with the resources and opportunity to freely choose how they play will empower them and give them self-confidence to explore and experiment.

### ✚ Health & Safety

Children must take care with rocks during small world play and should understand they are not to be thrown.

## What to do:

1. Collect small world pieces that link with the children's current interests.

2. The 'what you need' list is just an idea of things you may wish to include. Use whatever you can lay your hands on easily and try to create as many different surfaces and resources as you can to the children's small world play.

3. Use two tuff trays at differing levels to add variety and promote physical stretching and crouching during play.

4. Include a variety of jumbled small world pieces to allow the children to combine and bring worlds together in collaborative and imaginative play.

5. Use resources which range in size and scale to promote problem-solving skills. A child who cannot fit their dinosaur into the digger will display a range of emotions before solving the problem and continuing to play successfully.

6. Small world play will allow children the opportunity for independent play during which they should be able to explore freely. However, a supporting adult should be close by who may get invited into the child's play. This activity can be used to promote language development and help the children to expand on their own imaginative ideas.

7. Add items which the children can safely experiment with through their small world play. Add rocks and sticks for the children to explore how different actions leads to different outcomes, practising cause and effect safely without great consequences.

# Colour mixing
## Sand play

## What you need:

- Coloured play sand
- Soap dispensers with water
- Small pots and containers
- Teaspoons

## Top tip ⭐

Using only a small amount of sand with small pots and spoons will keep the exploration contained on the tuff tray. This will help the children focus more closely on the investigation.

### Taking it forward

- Leaving a little soap in the dispenser before adding the water will make the sand light and creamy and add another component to the sand investigation.

### What's in it for the children?

This is an activity which can promote awe and wonder as the colours and consistency of the sand changes. It is an opportunity to promote scientific language and for the children to make predictions and then experiment with their theories.

### ➕ Health & Safety

Always ensure that the children don't get sand in their eyes by supervising closely.

## What to do:

1. Place small piles of coloured sand in the tuff tray and spread the other resources around.
2. Talk to the children about the different colours and ask them to predict the colours they might create.
3. Discuss the texture of the sand and ask the children how they think it will change once wet.
4. Allow the children to explore and experiment using the water, small pots, containers and teaspoons.
5. Use the activity to promote conversation and scientific talk about cause and effect.

# Inclining tubes and reflections
## Sand play

## What you need:

- 2 tuff trays
- Mirror or reflective sheeting
- Sand
- Cardboard tubes
- Teaspoons
- Funnels
- Bowls
- Tape

## Top tip ★

Do not add too much sand. This activity promotes analysis and investigation through trial and error. It's about the transportation of sand and not about digging, filling or emptying.

## What to do:

1. Set up two tuff trays at different heights. Place the reflective sheet or mirror into the higher tuff tray.

2. Add mounds of sand around the tuff tray. You can use different colours and textures (some damp and some dry).

3. Provide tubes of different lengths and widths to promote investigation and challenge.

4. Tape three or four tubes together to create diversity of levels by positioning them so that they go from the higher tuff tray to the lower one.

5. Provide teaspoons which allow the children to put the sand directly down the tube for those who are unable to transfer the sand using the funnels.

6. Add the bowls for the children to add sand into, creating their own station in this shared exercise.

7. Allow the children to investigate freely.

8. Suggest that the children might mark make in the sand or play hide and seek by covering the mirror with sand and then removing it to reveal the reflection.

## Taking it forward

- Add plastic piping and drains and include water alongside the sand.

## What's in it for the children?

Children may explore mathematically by measuring the distance and speed the sand travels through the tubes or may experiment scientifically by comparing the way the different textures are transported. Some will mark make on the reflective surface or show curiosity about their reflections. The opportunity for language development is good as the children problem solve and investigate.

## ✚ Health & Safety

As with all sand activities, ensure that the children don't get sand in their eyes by supervising closely.

# Motion sand
## Sand play

**What to do:**

1. Place the loose parts in the centre of the tuff tray so that children can reach them easily.

2. Add the motion sand around the outside of the tuff tray.

3. Allow the children to explore and experiment with the sand and loose parts.

4. Talk with the children about the movement of the sand and discuss how this differs from regular sand.

5. Experiment with creating sculptures and talk about how the sand moulds easily into place.

## Top tip ★

Shop around online to find the best deal for the motion sand as it can be expensive. Store in an air-tight container.

### Taking it forward

- Why not include different resources to explore, or add the motion sand into small world provocations?

- Challenge the children to create specific objects with the motion sand or use shells to create 'fossil' impressions or paw prints with small world animals.

### What's in it for the children?

The children will enjoy the textures and the sensory play of this activity. Moulding and modelling is much more achievable with this durable sand and will provide the children with a sense of achievement.

### ✚ Health & Safety

Always ensure that the children don't get sand in their eyes by supervising closely.

# Sandy tights
## Sand play

## What you need:

- Spoons
- Scoops
- Scales
- Sand tray or bucket of sand
- Small children's tights
- Funnels

## What to do:

1. Prepare the tuff tray with a selection of tools for scooping and pouring for the children to choose from.
2. Add scales to the tuff tray so that the children can compare the weight of each leg of the sandy tights once they are filled.
3. Use either a bucket of sand or a sand tray for the children to fill their tights over.
4. Model how to fill the tights using funnels or spoons. Encourage children to work together to achieve their goal, e.g. one child holds the tights open as another spoons in the sand. Demonstrate what happens when you fill the tights; hold them at the waistband and observe how they walk and bounce along. If the sand is unequal, the lightest leg will bounce higher. Use this as an invitation to explore weights and quantity.
5. Allow the children to explore and experiment with their 'sandy tights'.

## Taking it forward

- Use a variety of sizes and colours of tights for the children to make comparisons.
- Try filling the tights with different materials and observe the effect this has on the movement.
- Add a rock to one leg of the tights and sand in the other to see how this impacts the movement.

## What's in it for the children?

This will provide problem-solving opportunities for the children as they decide on the best apparatus for filling the tights. There are many mathematical opportunities with this activity such as comparing volume, quantity and weight. It also requires developed physical skills for filling the tights such as good hand-eye coordination and, for moving the tights along once filled, upper arm muscle strength.

# Transporting sand
Sand play

## What you need:

- Cardboard box to fit into a tuff tray
- Tubes
- Pencil
- Sharp knife
- Sticky tape
- Sand
- Pots and pans
- Tools for transporting (spoons, dish brushes and scoops)

### Taking it forward

- Explore moving sand and other mediums vertically and diagonally using pipes and the tuff tray (see page 34).
- Compare using wet sand and dry sand, and allow the children to solve problems which may occur using the different textures.

### What's in it for the children?

This is an activity which promotes mathematical thinking as the children must negotiate space, size and distance along with direction. The children will choose the tools required to move the sand through the tubes which will also give them a sense of achievement and self-confidence when they achieve their goals.

### ✚ Health & Safety

There is a risk of one child looking through a pipe whilst another is poking an item through. The children should be pre-warned of this risk and encouraged to work together to ensure this does not happen.

## What to do:

1. On one side of the cardboard box, draw around one of the tubes and use a sharp knife to cut out a hole.
2. Use a ruler to measure where to draw a circle on the opposite side of the box. Make multiple holes.
3. Slide tubes into the holes to create a horizontal pipe through the cardboard box.
4. Tape around the holes to stop the tubes from being moved forwards and backwards.
5. Put the box in the tuff tray.
6. Provide sand and tools for the children to experiment with posting and moving through the tubes.
7. Place pots and pans on one side of the box to catch the sand.
8. Allow the children time to investigate and explore freely. The children must work out how to move the sand through the tubes and will develop critical thinking skills to solve the problem.

### Top tip ⭐

To explore 'vertical transportatio' simply turn the box on its side in the tuff tray so that sand can be posted downwards.